Praise for *All She Needs Is Love*

I cried my way through this collection of poetry, the good kind of tears, the kind that heal the soul. Evocative to the soul – these are the first words that came to me as I was reading the magic that is Amy's to express and touch us all where we most come together, a place where we are all far more alike than different. This is union. Union of soul and human, union of all souls and all humans collectively. This is love. Not the pretty picture you want love to be, but all of love honoured in every single one of its forms. I've been fortunate to witness Amy's enchanted manifestation unfold over many years. This is truly a culmination of her passion and her courage. A perfect intersection of awareness, expression, authenticity, honesty and of course love that will leave you in greater touch with yourself; in the most gentle of ways supporting the unfolding of your own love, of your own self. A glowing reminder "to thine own self be true". My wish to you, reader, is that like Amy's use of space in this, that you find your space to connect even more fully to yourself.

I leave this with you, her words, not mine, mixed and matched from her works:

Retreat into your fullness.
Love is your birthright.
Love is a FOCUS.
The love that runs through your veins is your medicine.
Freedom beholds.
After all, you've already arrived.
There was never anything for you to do but unfold into love.

All My Love,
~Allison Bachmeier, Transformation Specialist @ Vibrant Transformation

***

All She Needs Is Love is an amazing view of the world painted by someone that truly loves life while simultaneously feeling the deep soulful pain of existence.

As I read each page, each line of truth, I found my soul telling me to slow down and read that last line again. What began as the reading of a book quickly became an exploration of myself, a journey deep inside of me as I recognized my pain on the page in front of me.

For those of us who "stay away (from ourselves) because sometimes I don't even know what's truly me" Amy helps you see those shadows and meet them with the love they long for. You too will "meet the most exquisite nectar of (your) pain" and realize the time has come for you to love that pain and welcome every bit of yourself to join you in the light created by love.

I am sure you will, as I did, find that "her words are poetry that can move into the deepest of souls. Her art can provoke those willing to wake up to their greatness." All She Needs Is Love will have you realizing that you too "are in love with a woman"…and that woman is you.

~ Michael Barrett, Love Ambassador and High Performance Coach

***

Amy's intimate poetry, prose and spoken word collection *All She Needs is Love* is full of personal turmoil, reflection, and salvation. It's an epic library of encouragement, rallying and declaring a battle cry that we are worthy. Worthy of joy, peace, freedom and love.

The authenticity of the book's author is critical to understanding its blunt and honest poems. They express feelings of anxiety, hopelessness, isolation, and depression, charting frustrating attempts to pierce the dark shroud that encloses their narrator. The entries probe life experiences that are real, raw and relatable. Some poems suggest other topics, such as body image, waiting and power, but the underlying theme is a unified one, of making love loud. Piercingly loud.

Amy's style is direct, and many selections need but a few words to communicate her message, others take us on a journey where we see ourselves in the midst of her narrative. Amy's work is undeniably engaging, often because of her unapologetic transparency. This beautiful compilation will leave you breathless, introspective and full of hope. It will also bring you to an epiphany that all you need is love.

~Joe Altelig, Speaker, Personal Growth Coach, Founder of The Love Wave

***

Amy writes from her soul in a way that is authentic and relatable leaving the reader feeling heard and understood. The topics are real to life and are approached in a down to earth way connecting to emotions and experiences that many of us have moved through in life. *All She Needs Is Love* is a beautiful work of self realization and healing.

~ Tammy deLaforest

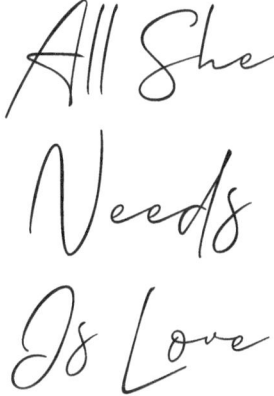

All She Needs Is Love

The Love You Are Seeking Is Within You

AMY DAWNS

Copyright ©2020 Amy Walls
Cover Design: Corto Maltese

Published by: Big Moose Publishing
PO Box 127 Site 601 RR#6 Saskatoon, SK CANADA S7K3J9
www.bigmoosepublishing.com

All rights reserved. No part of this book may be used or reproduced by any means, graphic, electronic, or mechanical, including photocopying, recording, taping or by any information storage retrieval system without the written permission of the author except in the case of brief quotations embodied in critical articles and reviews.

Because of the dynamic nature of the Internet, any web addresses or links contained in this book may have changed since publication and may no longer be valid. The views expressed in this work are solely those of the author(s) and do not necessarily reflect the views of the publisher, and the publisher hereby disclaims any responsibility for them.

The author(s) of this book does not dispense medical advice or prescribe the use of any technique as a form of treatment for physical, emotional, or medical problems without the advice of a physician, either directly or indirectly. The intent of the author is only to offer information of a general nature to help you in your quest for emotional and spiritual well-being. In the event you use any of the information in this book for yourself, which is your constitutional right, the author and the publisher assume no responsibility for your actions.

ISBN: 978-1-989840-14-6 (Paperback)
ISBN: 978-1-989840-15-3 (Ebook)

Big Moose Publishing 08/2020

To every woman, may you find permission in this collection of poetry, insights and provisions, to meet yourself where you are with radical love and acceptance.

To every man, may you see the women in your life through a new lens of love.

Life is a mirror.

You are worthy.

Contents

Acknowledgments...i
Foreword..iii
Introduction..vii
How to Use This Book x

SELF LOVE

Loving Fear..1
Beautiful Woman..9
Sweet One...14
Love Calls..16
Showing Up..48
Earth Angel...49
The Illusion of Perfection..51
The Importance of Rest..52
So What...68
Leap..69
In Love with a Woman..74
Take a Chance on Me...80
Spark...98
Divine Power...125

EMPOWERMENT

Part of My Story...3
Lost..17
Resilience..20
Holding Space...38
Power...90

Ambassador of Love..91

GRACE
Everything Is Happening for You...................................28
Emotional Release..32
God's Grace...33
Carried..35
Love Is a Focus...99
Broken Man..103
Sweet Surrender...106
Love Never Leaves...107
Let It Go..109
Brave Girl's Lullaby..115
Heaven's Scripture...118

HEALING
Icy Memories..5
Yesterday..6
It's Not a Race..7
Without..8
Marriage...15
This Season..21
When Nothing Works..23
Soul Cracks..25
All the Faces We Wear..29
Strength of Vulnerability...41
Releasing Shame..45
Wanting..70
Mind Chatter...73
The Guy that Couldn't Get the Girl................................78
Dear Money...81
Unspoken Wisdom..93
Potential...94

Presence..95
Longing..105
Dirt..112
Whatever...114
Peace..117
Divine Love...123

PATIENCE
Wait for This Kind of Love...2
Coming In..124

PRESENCE
Already There..11
Shadow..27
Flipping the Script..40
Space...53
Folding..55
The LEAP...76
Love Is Still the Answer..89
Into Me See...102
Beyond What You Know...108
Alignment..110
Courage...119
Guidance...120
Vulnerability...121
Intuition..122
Deep Down...126

WAITING
You're Not Here Yet..31
Pain of Desire..34
Love That's Meant for You.......................................42

SELF WORTH

Leaving Pretty..4
Roar..12
Wild Woman..18
The Weight We Carry..36
It's Not Your Job..37
When She Comes..43
Goddess's Garden...72
Money Responds...84
"No man is ever going to live up to your standards."............86
Embodiment..111

Acknowledgments

To my parents for choosing to bring me into this world. Thank you for teaching me that the core values we instill in our children don't ever get lost. They rise when we are developed enough. Thank you for teaching me that parents really do the very best with what they know and have. Thank you for doing your best and for loving me.

To my son for being the catalyst for transformation in my life. Thank you for giving me a voice that I had lost for so long, and for being my mirror and my master. I love you to infinity and beyond.

And to God, whose relationship has confused me at times, but always brought me back to the well of grace and mercy. Thank you for all the gifts you planted inside of me. My relationship with you continues to deepen and grow. I love you.

Thank you to life, my greatest testimony and my legacy. Thank you for showing me that it was always about love, it's always been about love and will continue to expand in love.

To my hurt, pain and trauma. The parts that have transformed and the parts that I still carry, I love you, I see you, I feel you and I hear you. Thank you for teaching me one of the most important values in life: compassion. You are my greatest spiritual guide.

To my joy, my light, and my divinity. Thank you for lighting the way when I couldn't see, for embracing me when I couldn't feel, for breaking through the cracks when I was broken and for lifting me when I felt heavy. Thank you for rising from the ashes time and time again and always standing in truth of what I really am.

Thank you to the one I see in the mirror. The one I still criticize. The one who locked eyes with me to see my own soul. The one who has reached peaks of bliss I can't even describe. The one who has come crashing down from those peaks and shed layers of unworthiness. To the one - the one I was always looking for each and every time. It was always you. You have been with me through it all. That is a sacred union. I see you Amy and I love you.

Foreword

I believe there is a book in all of us. We all have a story to tell. We all have experienced things that make a difference to this world and to others who live in this world. Unfortunately, for many of us, our stories are filled with dark things, shameful pasts, and experiences we would rather sweep under the rug than express in full glory on the blank page. Yet, it is going through these dark times that allow us to come more fully into the light.

Courage is being able to admit to yourself that it's okay to have lived what you have lived, no matter what it is you have lived. Denying it does nothing to heal the wounds and hurts we have come across along the way. Exposing it, not with the intention of punishing it, but instead acknowledging it without judgment, is what heals.

It never ceases to amaze me that when someone tells their story with honesty and vulnerability how great of an impact it has on others. I believe this is because we are essentially all the same. We think we are alone in our struggles until we read that another has gone through something similar. We think we will be cast aside for not being perfect until we realize everyone has the same fear. When one person has the courage to break through that fear and tell their deepest, darkest secrets without casting themselves aside, it gives permission for another to come clean with themselves and accept themselves for the beauty and glory they truly are.

I have written a few books and have shared intimate stories within them, and each time, I was worried that somehow, once the world found out the truth about me, that they would surely shun me. Yet, each time the exact opposite has occurred. People have come forward and opened up to me. They have shared their stories and found relief in doing so. They have embraced me, thanked me, loved me, and honoured me when I was so scared that they would judge me, belittle me, reject me, and hate me. This is what fear does. It makes us believe things that aren't true, and it keeps us from the magnificent gifts that can be bestowed upon us when we just be honest about ourselves.

Writing has always been therapeutic to me. I have been blessed with the ability to communicate effectively through prose. It is my art form. In this book, Amy also exemplifies being an artist with words, but in a different way. While prose is my medium, poetry is hers. She expresses herself and her story with beauty, grace, and a raw honesty through poetic verse. I invite you to let each line sink in and give meaning to you in whatever way that comes. It will come differently to each person.

Art, no matter the medium in which it is delivered, invokes feelings, emotion, and awareness of self. Words are art. Within you there are beautiful masterpieces. Let them out even if it is just in a diary or on a scrap piece of paper. You have volumes within that all have value in being expressed.

You may find in the expression of them that you come to see the value, beauty, and magnificence of you.

I hope you enjoy this book as much as I have. There is so much depth of emotion placed on each page that something is sure to hit home. Let it. And if pain surfaces, be brave enough to let it be expressed. Pain is a very creative energy when we are willing to allow for it. Through that allowance the pain transforms into something beautiful – it transforms into art. If you start to view your pain as a creative force that can reveal your beauty, your life will be something that you will want to create with, not hide from.

Enjoy the journey of self-realization and self-expression. You may just fall in love with yourself, with your life, with everything.

Fay Thompson
Author of So Help Me God, Inspirations for a Brighter Day Volumes I &II, and Azez Medicine
Editor-in-Chief at Big Moose Publishing

Introduction

I believe now more than ever with the rise of silent suffering coming into conscious awareness, that we need more LOVE both from ourselves and each other. As more women boldly step forward acknowledging their trauma, pain, and truth that have been silently contained in their bodies, the world as we know it is changing. For many of us, we have learned to contain our trauma from so many generations past.

I want to acknowledge all of you who are bravely stepping into the courage of your hearts and allowing your pain to be felt, heard, and seen in your own time and your own way. This is no easy feat and requires a lot of compassion and grace. It is truly about meeting yourself where you are.

After experiencing a lot of trauma throughout my life, I have spent many years diving deep into the trenches of my soul. Trauma has a way of sneaking up on you when you least expect it. Even after all these years of some of the deepest healing work, I am still uncertain if trauma will ever really "go away". It surely has dissipated and become more detached from the truth of what I am. This book isn't a promise that your pain, trauma, or suffering will "go away". It is, however, an invitation and permission into a safe place for you to be held and to experience fully where you are right now. It is a place to be seen, heard, and loved for all that you have gone through and are currently going through. It is a place where you can connect collectively to others who feel the same as you, and to remind yourself that you are not alone. It is a place where your feelings are valid and they don't make you any less of a woman. In fact, I truly believe that after having been through all that you've been through, you are a strong, courageous, and worthy woman.

This book is much like an oracle - an opening to a way inside yourself - into the mystery and beauty of who you are where all the love that you've been looking for resides. Even if you don't always feel this love, or maybe have never felt this love before, keep your heart open to this possibility as you dive into this book. Love is underneath all of the trauma and pain; this I can promise, at least from my own experiences of meeting myself where I am, meeting my clients where they are, and having others meet where I am in return. There is nothing quite like this beautiful expression of love.

This book is a collection of poems, insights, and provisions expressing myself sincerely and authentically, where I was in the moment. It is raw and real, and although it is not the "perfect" image of love that we are used to "seeing", it is the purest unfolding of a perfect love story with myself. Writing is a form which I can safely and unapologetically express what I'm "growing" through, what I have learned, and what I do not yet know. You can expect all emotions in this book to be found. I hide nothing; love hides nothing.

We carry so much within and I truly feel we are being called to free and reveal what's inside. Everything within you is honourable. What if you just needed permission to unload into a space where there will be no judgment? This book is a means for that. I have even included blank pages in the very core of this book so that you can let it all go right here. Hold nothing back. Let it all out - every single thought, feeling, and sensation. Your tears are welcome here. Your anger is welcome. The WHOLE of you is welcome, right here. It's a really great way to release some of the heaviness we carry inside. Welcome every thought and every emotion. It's okay to cry and it's safe to feel. Allow this to purify what's been held so that it can be released. It's okay to vocalize other ways as well. Your very nature is wild and free. Allow this part of you to rise.

How to Use This Book

This book is not set up linearly. I did this with purpose, because life is not linear as much as we like to think it is. It has peaks and valleys, highs and lows which need to be honoured. You could read it front to back; that isn't wrong. Or you could jump to a page that you're drawn to based on a theme that is speaking to you. You could even just randomly open a page and read it that way. Remember, I said this book acts like an oracle, so meet yourself where you are and ask yourself what is calling to you.

There is also a lot of empty space in this book for a reason. Space is something that has enriched my life. Space to breathe, space to step back and reflect, space to retreat and go within, space to hold myself as I can feel a trauma story rising, and space for all of me to be seen, heard, and loved. So please, use this space. Write on it, draw on it, and do whatever you want to do with this space. Focus on it too. It's a great tool for when we are feeling overwhelmed because when we are focusing on our problems, we tend to forget about all the space that is around us. This is your book. It is in your hands. There are no rules, only the intuitive leads of your own heart.

As a suggestion to anchor more deeply into your heart before reading, close your eyes and place one hand over your heart, take a couple of deep breaths in and out. Ask yourself this question quietly, "What is available for me to receive right now?"

Wait for the answer. It will come.

In the center of this book you will find 12 blank pages as an invitation to come back to your center - to the core of who you are. The center is indicated by a rose-filled page and the poem "Folding". You can find this on Page 55.

Each blank page has a question at the top. The questions are an invitation for you to empty yourself onto these pages. They are permission for your pure expression in whatever form it shows up in; words, poetry, feelings, drawing, etc.; they are your pages for you to unfold into. The more you can empty yourself, the more spaciousness you will feel. Sink deeply into the embrace of the pages. Become the rose, let the petals fall away one by one until you are simply here, experiencing and witnessing yourself.

I love you.

Be kind and loving towards yourself like you're the best thing that's ever happened for you, because you are.

It's time.

You've never been more ready to start loving all of you.

Loving Fear

Maybe it's not about being fearlessly bold.
Maybe it's about being fearfully bold.
Maybe it's about being ok with all your insecurities.
And all your imperfections.
Acknowledging that you still don't like things about yourself.
You still struggle with confidence and self esteem.
And maybe that is what is bold.
Having the courage not to try to present yourself a certain way.
But instead showing up fearfully you.
A little shaky inside.
A little doubtful.
A little anxious still.
Maybe that's what builds confidence.
Not trying to be anything other than you are at the moment.
And being honest when you are trying to be something other than you are.
I think of this little kid inside of me.
She still wants approval.
She still wants people to love her.
She still wants to be accepted and validated.
So, there is in some way this little fear that steps with me every time I put myself out there.
And hopes that I will be respected,
Wanted,
Appreciated.
I'm okay with that.
Because every time I step out I bring fear with me.
I let it be seen.
I let it be heard.
So that it can be loved.
And I am giving you permission to do the same.

Wait for This Kind of Love

We don't fall in love with people; we fall in love with their perspectives.

And, essentially, if two people fall in love with each other's perspectives, and I'm talking about perspectives that reach so deeply into your heart that it sends a signal to every single cell of your body and it opens pathways to the mind,

And these harmonizing perspectives collide in such a way that it creates a vortex, a paradigm shift in the way they view the world,

Where life is expanded and fed from the source of the great spirit,

These perspectives become the spiritual form in which love can transcend through time and space and all realities.

To create something new and so vital that new things grow there, and when any perspectives show up that are not in harmony with this new creation, they will in fact be the stomping grounds for all healing, and all limitations placed within the vessel of the human personality,

And exponentially transform the world and their partnership.

A life-enhancing partnership where love is the source and the root of transcendence.

This is the kind of love I'm waiting for.

Part of My Story

What you don't realize is
all those times I felt love from a man
At some point I thought about you.
All the times I let myself open to being felt, seen and desired
You came up eventually in a conversation.
I've spoken about you my whole life.
I've told the story, so these men who chose to love me, maybe wouldn't hurt me like you did.
You have been a part of my tale, less the fairy, for so long.
It's almost like a worn out blanket that doesn't keep me warm.
Nor safe.
Every time I revealed you to them.
You lost your power.
And although they hurt me anyways
I slowly started hurting myself less.
By the way in which your clammy wet hands melted off my lips.
And your hand that slid up my thigh, dripped from my skin.
Every time I spoke, I released you more
Until you no longer were a part of me.
What you don't realize
Is you may have been part of my story
But my power lies in the way I can live fully and still speak about you without giving any of my power away.

Leaving Pretty

I quit.
I'm done.
It's not my job.
Someone gave it to me.
I don't even remember who.
I just know I've wasted so much time.
Spent so much energy.
And money.
On this job I didn't even ask for.
You see, this isn't who I am.
It's who you think I need to be.
I don't need to put on masks anymore.
For you to like me.
Accept me.
Love me.
And approve me.
I approve me.
So this is my final resignation.
I'm quitting.
This soul sucking job.
And yes I'm taking my inheritance.
My soul inheritance of vitality.
Beauty and bliss.
Authenticity and uniqueness.
Quirkiness and weirdness.
Wild and free.
So don't ask me to come back.
Because nothing you could offer me.
Could make me fall for your manipulative schemes.
This is my resignation.
Once and for all.
I'm leaving pretty.

Icy Memories

Every time you touched me I wanted to surrender.
But the memory of being touched is etched in my skin.
It's twisted in my innocence.
To be touched is to be loved.
But I was touched by darkness.
And robbed of my purity.
Much too young.
And now you are here touching me.
And I want to release into its warmth.
So I don't feel his ice inside me anymore.

Yesterday

It seems like only yesterday
Because yesterday still lives in your tears.
And your tears release like a waterfall that floods your today.
And tomorrow is an escape of the drowning
A flee from your existence.
And you will do anything not to exist in the pain of all the yesterdays that feel like today.
The eternal memories that you wish you could erase from your heart and mind forever.
Only to find you empty.
Longing for more.

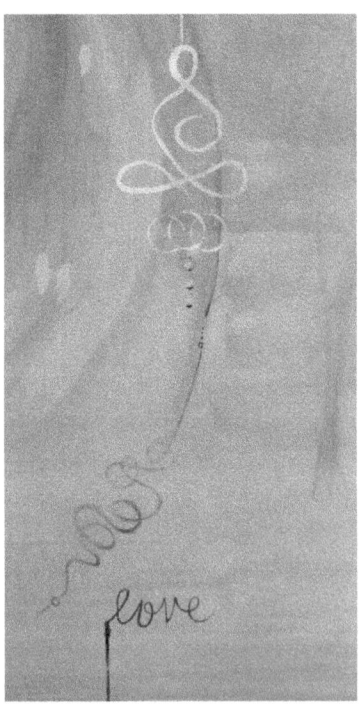

It's Not a Race

Spirituality isn't a race.
It's not a competition to win some high achievement.
It's connection.
You can taste its essence in many forms.
But the minute you think yours tastes better
You've lost connection.
The minute you say your way to spiritual awakening is the way,
you've lost connection.
Don't become so spiritually egoic you forget the true nature of divine connection.
In our search for becoming more spiritually connected we can become spiritually complacent.
We can begin to hand over all of reasoning to the universe.
And spiritual complacency has created its own set of belief systems.
When we are in flow living moment to moment, connected and conscious to our inner being, we will be in sync with the universe.
And it's great.
But using the universe to mask what we're not owning, we need to become aware that we are using a spiritual excuse to dismiss our truth.
We are still living and acting from the illusion that we are not naturally spiritual.
That we are not God Given.
Chosen.
When we are the universe.
And God is inside of us.
We need to own our decision making.
Each and every time.

Without

We are born completely without.
Without clothes.
Without a cloth to wipe our blood.
Without the ability to see where we are.
Without any knowledge.
And yet everything we need is right there for us.
And we are seen.
All eyes are on us.
All of the attention is on us.
When we are born we are in the spotlight.
And we don't have anxiety.
We don't think, oh my god, we are naked!
We don't know any other way yet.
So let me ask you this.
All the ways that you have learned since then, how are they working for you?
Can you still be in the spotlight and completely comfortable with everyone looking at you?
Do you have anxiety when it comes to being completely without?
Do you feel love when all eyes are on you?
Do you think oh my God, I am naked and exposed?
Every single moment we are being asked to step into the spotlight.
We are being nudged to be completely naked and exposed.
To be vulnerable and feel loved just for being us.

So unlearn. Reveal. Transform.
That is becoming something you have never been before and it will require a BRAND NEW WAY.
One that was born with you.
That birthed you.
It's incredible.
It's yours and it's meant for you.

Beautiful Woman

Let your belly hang out. Eat some chocolate.
Caress the parts on your body that get neglected because you don't like them.
Massage them. Caress them gently. Use warm oils.
Nurture your badass self.
Spend more time naked.
No matter what your body looks like.
Dedicate naked time daily/weekly/monthly.
Crank up the heat.
Don't put clothes on during this time of devotion.
Soak up the energy and let your body that's always covered up, breathe.
Dance naked. Text naked.
Do it all naked.
Just for you.
Have a heart to heart with your HEART.
Sit down in front of a mirror. Acknowledge you are here.
Meeting yourself as you are, maybe naked.
Take some slow deep breaths.
Get into your heart. Don't run away.
Be okay with it feeling awkward and emotional.
Start talking to yourself from your heart.
What does it have to say?
Forgive. Forgive. Forgive.
Beautiful woman.
Any thought that doesn't make you feel good holds judgment.
And that judgment plants a garden of grudges.
Thoughts that make you feel ill and resentful.
Forgive. Release those emotions of illness.
Forgive again. And again. And again.
Let the release happen.
Bless yourself.

Thank yourself for being here.
For doing all that you do. For showing up like this.
As you are.
Bless your environment. Bless your pets and plants.
All the things that you own.
Bless your bank account. Bless your car.
Bless your phone and Facebook.
Bless this moment.
Bless your future.
Bless your past.
Say thank you that today you had a moment to take out just for you.
To see you for all that you are.

Already There

You've already arrived.
Now the question is, will you enjoy it?

Amy Dawns

Roar

Woman, when did you start playing small?
When was the first time you questioned your confidence?
When was the first time you sucked in your belly?
When was the first time you looked in the mirror and wanted to cover it up because you didn't feel pretty enough?
When did you first dress for someone else?

Woman, when was the first time you tamed your roar?
When did you power down your laugh?
When did you stop your dance right in the middle of a glance?

When was the first time you stopped playing full out?

You were born with a roar not needing to be tamed.
A laugh so powerful it could penetrate men's hearts.
A face that can illuminate the entire universe.
A body strong, beautiful, and fucking organic.

You were not born a robot.
You were not born to be programmed by anything less than goddess.
Anything less than you.

So I ask you once more.
Woman, when was the first time you started playing small?
Go back and fetch her.
Go back and hold her.
Go back and cheer her on so loudly that her roar penetrates your heart.

Wildly
Free
ROAR

LOUDLY
PROUDLY
VICARIOUSLY
UNAPOLOGETICALLY

And commit from this day
To never ever play small again.

Sweet One

Oh sweet one.
The sweetness of life is everywhere.
It is not something you lose.
Or something to fear.
It is not something that is prized by how well you are doing with your life.
It is the very fragrance you lay your breath upon.
It is the voice that speaks to you when you are sad.
It is in the subtle chime in the wind and the electric breeze of a birds chirp.
It's everywhere and in all things.
It is abundant for you to experience anytime and anywhere that you allow yourself permission to taste it's sweet, desiccant song.
There is nothing for you to fix to receive its gracious offering.
Life is sweet.
It is meant for you.
Let it lead you to ecstasy.
And the grove of pure honey
Where your nectar and its liquid love become one.
Sweet sweet one

Marriage

Maybe the problem isn't that our marriage failed. Maybe the problem is in the pathology of the story being told. The story that "my marriage failed" can carry with it so much intense, heavy, dense energy and emotions. What if marriages don't fail just because they end?
We don't look at a tree that's losing its leaves and say it failed to keep its leaves.
We don't look at a dog that needs to put down and say it failed at living.
Humans are the only species to look at what they're doing as failure.
We look at people who commit suicide and come to the conclusion that they failed to love themselves enough.
We look at people whose marriages fall apart and come to the conclusion they failed to keep it together.
The pathology is in the story telling.
The perception is in our own conclusions.
My marriage ended.
My marriage was successful because I choose to see it that way. There was so much love, growth, expansion, and evolution that came from my marriage.
Just like everything changes with each season, our marriage moved to separation.
We still have a partnership.
Which I feel is the success of the marriage.
That didn't end.
It only transformed.
It's still growing and evolving and loving.

Love Calls

My wish for you is when you become so entangled with the stories that your mind creates, that love calls you.
And you hear it.
Or recognize it.
May love show up in the form of a smile from a stranger.
Or a song that plays on the radio.
Or a group healing that you attend.
Or the wind that for a moment it's breeze makes you forget everything.
Or your child that laughs.
Or your dog that cuddles with you.
Or the person that holds the door open for you.
Or the setting of the sun.
Because love never leaves.
It is always there.
And just because you become entangled, does not make you less deserving of love.
Love is your birthright.
You are love.
May you come to experience it over and over again in your life that one day you recognize yourself as it.

Lost

At any age you may become lost.
And who is lost knows nothing.
And knowing nothing means you get to start over.
Be born again and learn everything new.
The next stage of your life can be the best damn time of your life if you choose to see it as an opportunity to explore, learn and embrace life.
You don't need to put it all together.
Everything is already all put together.
You weren't born saying,
"I'm lost. Shit. Now I've gotta figure my life out."
You were born and you opened your eyes and were like,
"Wow! This is fucking awesome."
You already know who you are.
It's everything that you are not.
The only thing you have to do is explore every day like it's brand new.
And get out of your head and into life.
That is the journey.

Wild Woman

Dear Wild Conscious Awakened Woman:

The one that was molested, raped, abused when you were innocent.
I'm speaking to you.
This invasion of your perfect body.
The attack on your spirit.
The probing of your mind.
The one who froze in fear.
The one who withdrew and curled up into a ball.
The one that couldn't speak.
I want you to know. You did it perfectly.
The built in innate intelligence of your young innocence
When you are under invasion is to withdraw.
It's the most natural form of self protection you had. You protected yourself.
I know society is trying to mess with your mind.
It's trying to brainwash you into thinking at that age, you could have defended yourself any differently.
They are liars.
You protected yourself in the most nurturing way, and you've never lost this ability to protect yourself.
Withdrawal can be the best form of protection from your environment.
Withdrawal is a way of respecting yourself when it is impossible for you to demand protection and respect from someone else.
And that brings me to now.
This conscious, stunning, gorgeous, powerful, awakened, wild woman you have become.
It is still okay to withdraw when you need to protect your heart, mind, body and soul.
It is okay to demand respect, and to know your non-negotiable

values.
It is okay to declare them.
It is okay to walk away from anyone who would try to invade your values and your morals.
You do not owe them anything.
You owe yourself and your well being everything.
It is more than okay to declare exactly who you are boldly.
You don't always have to be soft. You have a soul on fire.
A heart that is capable of loving the whole world.
You don't have to settle for anyone that does not respect your values and your needs to have a healthy, harmonious partnership.
You are just as strong in your withdrawal and self respect as you are in your declaration.
The man in harmony with you will be willing to tune into your emotions, tap into your raw wisdom, and tune into your mind and body with absolute respect and consideration.
If you retreat, retreat into your fullness.
Not into your smallness.
Because you are a BOLD, Delicate, Graceful, Loud, Beautiful, Plain, Gorgeous, Heroic, Nurturing, Free...

INCREDIBLE AMAZING WILD WOMAN!

Resilience

Your heart's hurting and it's validation that something amazing is on the horizon.
For every time you've been abandoned.
Every time you've felt completely left alone.
When you needed someone the most.
It was creating resilience in you.
Strength in you to discern that when your time comes, you will know without doubt what it feels like when someone is all in.
All in your life and your messy heart.

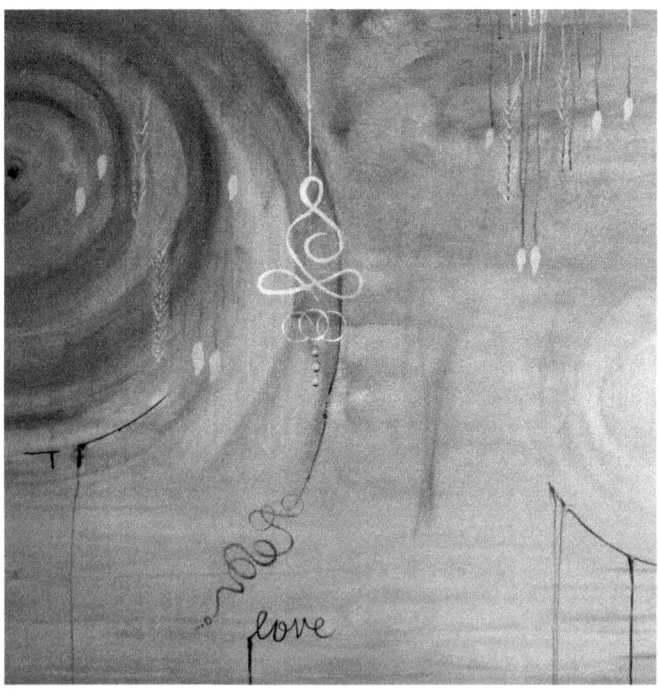

This Season

May all your worries dissolve with compassion,
And your resentments be forgiven by grace.
May you sit within the vessels of your heart,
And release the need to win this race.
Be still sweet one as the nectar beckons you deep within.
And one by one breath, you will win.
The divine is all around you and is singing you to sleep.
A peaceful slumber to recharge you and take you and your everlasting companionship deep.
Let it seep into your cells, your blood and your mind.
Let it allow you to heal and rejuvenate with kind.
It will call you by love and kindness so broad.
Here you will know that you're safe and protected from fraud.
The fraud of doubt and fear will cease to exist.
As you move into joy and happily ever after bliss.
Within your soul,
Within your heart,
Within your mind be still.
And listen ever so closely,
For the next inspired will.
You are love.
You are needed.
You are incredibly soft.
That is your gift.
This is your loft.
Curl up now and let love wrap you in its embrace.
To sleep, to sleep now.
In this heavenly space.
You will awake with young eyes and a youthful heart.
A full well of vitality to begin again, to start.
And this next cycle is calling your name.
This season.
This process will not be the same.

Amy Dawns

It is yours to receive.
Yours to allow.
Go and be still.
This is it.
This is now.

When Nothing Works

I couldn't reason it.
Analysis was not working.
Logic made it feel hard.
Lost. Looking For an answer.
The light clarity
As to why
What
When
How
Feeling all the motions.
Sick by every morsel of thought.
Seeping deeper into the abyss
I don't know
Scribbles
Illegible
Caving in
So tired
Nothing left.
Questioning everything.
And when I least expected it
So much cliche
Burning sage
Sat nam
Music playing
Hands at heart center
Crying an ocean of tears
How many oceans are within me?
All of them
and the seas.
There it was looking for me.
Embrace.
It was so simple.

Complete strangers
Embracing me
Holding me
Loving me.
Feeling the shame seep from me
Why
Would
Complete
Strangers
Embrace
Me
In my raw vulnerability?
And I saw it.
The essence of it.
The embrace and what it provided.
The same vital life giving energy that babies need fresh out of the womb
Naked
Messy
Raw
Crying
They can't live without it.
9 weeks of birthing
Fresh out of the woman
At my most vulnerable
And I needed the same.
Touch is essential.
I don't even need to be understood
Only to be embraced by people who know what love is.
We all need people.
There are many
Who have and fail to embrace
Giving shallow hugs
Afraid of going deep.
Shame wavering beneath
Touch
The one human sense we can't live without.
Not for long anyways.
Embrace.

Soul Cracks

I am a big piece of squishiness spread all too thin over the pavement.
Making waves through the cracks of my soul.
Waiting for water to flow.
I'm dried up or too moist. I'm uncertain as life takes things that no longer serve me.
Removed from lower parts of me.
Set me free.
But wait, what about me?! I wait.
There is not time or constraint to piece me back together.
That's not what this is about.
Yes I'm weathered to the bones. Made of stones.
Stop throwing them at me. Wait....that's me.
Release me.
Pick me up.
Cradle me in your arms for so long this storm has come and swept me off my feet and my ass to crash my insides that clash with my outsides.

Pieces of me scattered everywhere like hail that makes dents creating despair in my heart. Start.
Breathe.
Again.
Deeper.
Keep-her.
Love her.
Undone is what's done.
All she needs is love.
Reflected as the sun rises and the rainbows subtle hues melt into the backdrop of the sky or is it her heart that's melting back into colors vivid and brightly from her feet...
rise up to catch her from feeling beat down to the ground.

Grounding and earthing, dancing and flying.
This is all she needs.
The perfect storm settling itself into perfection making way for direction.
The path of infection of love like cotton candy on a stem swirled within her skin, deep within as she unraveled and traveled to the next level, the next layer of her human opened spirit wounded journey.

Shadow

I am not here to master myself. I am here to understand why I keep running away from my own reflection.

Everything Is Happening for You

This isn't heartache.
I am not shattered.
My tears weren't scattered.
They were cupped by the ocean.
And carried deep.
Transformed to treasures to keep.
The rising.
Of something extraordinary.
A fire that burns so fiercely and brightly.
I can't help but see it.
And there you are dancing like the King you are.
I did not have to do anything
But feel the burn
Of what wasn't meant for me.
I did not love too much.
Or expand beyond capacity.
I was practicing defying gravity.
I wasn't too much.
Or too small.
I was being moved in a glorious direction is all.
This wasn't the burn of the fire
Or of the sun
But of your desire.
Of our time come.
Where we dance as one.
I landed here right on time.

All The Faces We Wear

Yesterday I had a pretty face.
It was happy.
Beautiful.
Sexy.
So I showed you.
I gave you what you wanted.
For a temporary pause
In the stillness of ignorance
Life seemed perfect.

Yesterday I had a pretty face.
That you adored.
Loved.
Kissed.
So I let you.
I gave you what you wanted.
For a glimpse of feeling wanted.
And feeling loved.

Yesterday I had a pretty face.
That you touched.
And looked at as though,
I was the one
For you.
And for a moment
It felt like that was true.

Today, I took the pretty face off.
And put it in my closet.
With the rest of my masks.
And for a moment I felt
Exposed.

Amy Dawns

Raw.
Ugly.

Today I don't have any face.
It's gone
With you.

You're Not Here Yet

Sometimes I rest my head upon your imagined shoulder.
Pre-exercising you into existence.
I feel resistance
To the belief that one day you'll come.
Perhaps now you may be here.
And it is not yet recognizable.
Because I'm too bonded by fear.
Ideas I have are far out-reached.
Yet I feel when I lay here like this.
The mist clears and the fog lifts.
Just to sense my wishes held in my heart.
The love that I have for you is real and true and has not hardened
by words yet not spoken.
Like a token of affection I feel your touch not yet touched.
Your lips kissed like a soft rose petal on my skin.
Your fragrance lives in my breath and blossoms my heart open to
you without you even here yet.

Emotional Release

You're allowed to have those eyes swollen shut from crying all night; you don't need to explain yourself when it carries through to the morning darling. Rest your head, let your heart bare its skin. It's okay, you did nothing wrong. Give yourself the attention you are seeking. Today sweetness, wrap your emotions in a warm bath and let the tears trickle to God.

God's Grace

And like all the times she spilled her words into blood not a word was spoken, not a gesture of repent made.
Grace, she discovered, was in tears of blood that were laid before her and, because of that, she gave up the need for recognition and apologies from the masses. Because what lay in her heart's scriptures was God's remarkable calling to a greater cause.

Pain of Desire

I stand victim to the one who's hurting me from not being here yet.
The ache I feel is the love that's so large and waiting for you.
It's like grieving your soul mate after they die except the reverse.
Death first, then the physical manifestation of you.
Feeling your vibration is enough until I doubt it and fall away.
You reach a point in your life where you can feel the vibration but you cannot physically touch.
And your physical body aches because it wants to catch up to the energetic level with everything you are.

I stand victim to the one who's hurting me from not being here yet. It's like grieving your soul mate after they die except the reverse.
Death first, then the physical manifestation of you.

Carried

As Light As A Feather...

Who you really are is bigger than you can see from the ground.

That's the thing about your highest calling.

It will lift you up as high as an eagle can soar.

And, if you're hanging onto everything that keeps you on the ground,

You won't make it.

Let go of heavy.

So that light can lift you to the vast skies.

Where infinite possibilities lie.

Amy Dawns

The Weight We Carry

I once looked at you and thought you were me.
Identified with your ugly.
It made me feel safe and sound.
Where growing tall was death to where I would be buried underground.
And parts are for cars and automobiles. And I am not made up of steel.
I am made of transmutable clay.
That can melt away, with a sheer sense of love,
The pain of what I once thought I was.
My body is not a car, nor a well-oiled machine.
It is heaven wrapped in itself, waiting to be seen.
Yes there are mechanics of how it works. But those mechanisms are made of magical earth.
My body does not determine my worth.
So the next time you look at me and all you see
Is a body made up of judgments by what you've been conditioned to believe.
Know that I won't enable you're looking glass and your small scaled sight.
I'm not responsible for your fight.
Yes you have wings just like me,
and if I stay small, how are you ever to set yourself free?

It's Not Your Job

It's not your job to look sexy.
You can if you want.

It's not your job to dress to suit your suitor.
You can dress how you want.

It's not your job to love all of your body equally.
You can love it however you want.

It's not your job to make people like you.
You can do whatever you want.

It's not your job to make people follow you.
Post whatever you want.

Stop making living your life a job.
Stop making being YOU a chore.
Live the way you want.

Are you doing absolutely everything you want?

Holding Space

Dear girl with the 6 inch waist and 16 inch thighs.

To the girl who tucks her skin in between her legs so nothing hangs out.

To the mom whose children have climbed on her and she has screeched in pain when they accidentally put all of their weight on the extra trims of fat around the edges of her hips and thighs.

To the girl that has one ankle bigger than the other. And one calf that's fatter.

To the woman that won't wear shorts in public because she doesn't want anyone to see what's happened to her legs since losing all that weight. Gravity has given her loose skin and she feels ashamed that something so good that she's proud of accomplishing, still keeps her hiding.

To the woman with varicose veins that makes her feel older than you are.

To the girl whose knees limit her from dancing.

To the lady who feels trapped inside her body and wants to escape.

To the girl who constantly is searching for an answer and deeply grieves in silence, "Why doesn't my body match who I am on the inside?"

To the girl with the clusters of cellulite that she despises and wishes she could get rid of.

To the girl with stretch marks that hasn't even had a child and thinks there's something wrong with her because she didn't earn them.

To the girl that lost use of her legs and is paralyzed from the waist down.

To the girl who had one or both of her legs amputated to save her life.

To the girl who has wished she could have brand new legs and has felt guilty because she doesn't love the ones she has.

And she knows it could be worse.

I see you. I feel you. I love you.

May we all rise together.
Stronger than we ever knew.
Using the strength of our legs that have carried us through.
Let's learn to love them and accept them just as they are.
You are worth it.
You're amazing.
You've come this far.

Take one small step towards the truth in your heart.
Let this be a brand new chapter.
A new start.

You were made for greatness
Regardless of the body you're in.
You are beautiful.
You are free.
Let your new life begin.

Amy Dawns

Flipping the Script

Maybe when we don't feel fully in our body it's because our body is fully in us.

Strength of Vulnerability

Living vulnerably and feeling fully might appear to be a difficult way to live, because it requires a lot of courage to face the fears of the mind. One by one as you face each fear, you cut through the veils of illusion. You free yourself from the fears you created that bound you to life and allow life to flow through you, enamoured by the grace of beauty.

Love That's Meant for You

And one day someone is going to come and love you so big that you will forget the feeling of ever being left behind.

When She Comes

When she comes.

Get to know every detail of her.

Want to want to know every scar and each story they tell. This is where her strength comes from. It is the wisdom of her most sacred feminine.

Feel her laughter. Don't just listen, but allow it to vibrate through you.

Allow her to become the most vulnerable in your presence by being vulnerable in your own.

See her emotions as energy in motion. Energy that carries her through challenges, intensifies wonder, and moves her forward.

Let her tears fall when they are inspired to fall. These are the waves of her soul needing to be expressed. They are holy in nature and a beautiful rainfall of purification. Never stop her body's/mind's natural purification.

Be expressive in your own emotions authentically. She wants to know that you aren't afraid to feel.

Carry integrity and honour when you're with her. Be a man of your word followed by inspired action.

Be soft, never forceful.

Get to know every detail of her body. Kiss every inch of her including what she considers the ugliest parts of her. If you continue to touch her in this way eventually she will love these parts of her that she's been trying so hard to love all these years. You will have shown her her own strength by touching her in this way.

Touch her like it's the first time you are discovering her. Feel her like you've known her your whole life and want her to know how much you love her as if this was the last moment you had with her.

Never take away her rest, retreat, and rejuvenation. Healing happens in stillness and she needs this time like a fish needs water. It is vital for her womanly well-being.

Love her mind and just as you would touch her body, touch each corner of her mind. She wants to know you aren't afraid of depth and intellectual stimulation.

Touch her spirit. This is the heart of her soul. She is here because of this. Get to know your own spirit so you can feel what a soul connection is.

Tell her things. Everything. Even those things that make you afraid to say. Tell them softly yet boldly. Look right into her eyes. Save those things for face to face.

Write love letters. Pour your heart out in a letter as if this was your only way of communicating and it took time to get to her. Imagine the smile on her face when she reads it. The tears that glimmer in her eyes because she is feeling your words connect deep into her heart.

Court her like a queen; her body and mind are a royal temple. Each time you are in her presence you are among lush velvet wholeness.

Love her passion. It's her oxygen.

Love her contrast. Without it you would not see her beauty.

When she comes you will know. Trust this pure alignment that brought your souls together.

Releasing Shame

POOR OLD ME

She is alive still
He is too.
Within the bindings of the books that are stored in your heart.
In both of you.

Poor....
Small
Insignificant
Lacking
Bad
Imperfect
Insufficient
Inferior
Weak
Needy
Wrong
Invisible
Strapped
Broke
Wanting
Alone
Cheap
Cheesy
Gross
Icky
Inadequate
Lousy
Off
Sad
Garbage

Trash
Dirt

The bindings so old they creek like an abandoned and neglected hinge.
The dust so thick you have to peel it off to see what's underneath, the covers fringed.
Hiding
Waiting
For someone to finally notice its burial.

Old....
Tired
Broken Down
Decrepit
Inactive
Wasted
Past
Suppressed
Unspoken
Quiet
Weary
Brittle
Fragile
Neglected
Deteriorated
Rundown
Frail
Worn
Unsound

So gently opening its pages unfound. Stories of her and him, poor and old. And me waiting for the story to be told and I to unfold.

Me...
Single
Alone
Companionless

Scared
Friendless
Abandoned
Deserted
Isolated
Forsaken
Lonely
Unaccompanied
Sold

Slowly the dust lifts and the words levitate from the pages.
They dance and are free from the poor old stages.
And I release her and him.
Nothing poor, nothing less, nothing more
Simply
I AM

Showing Up

The only reason we don't show up is because we have a pre-conditioned idea of how we should.
When we could be showing up unconditionally in everything we do.
And we would actually feel way more fulfilled.
And FREE.

Earth Angel

I am an earth angel.
And I am meant to fly.
My feet only touch the ground to remind me that Mother Earth is my sacred ground.
The universe takes things from me that no longer align with my highest truth.
Sometimes that feels like extreme loss.
And leaves me questioning why I have wings.
If I have nowhere to go
What is the point?! I ask.
And I hear nothing but stillness after the question.
It's so loud it makes me want to run.
I try to run to catch the wind.
To lift my center
And connect with my wings.
I run harder.
And longer and faster.
But it doesn't work.
Why are you keeping me suction-cupped here!
I scream to mother.
Why give me wings when I cannot fly?!!!
There's no freedom in that!!!
My anger roars like a lioness that has lost her first-born cub.
My heart rips wide open like it's never seen daylight before.
Why have you taken it all from me?
Everything that ever gave me a sense of freedom.
I am a failure without freedom.
And I stomp entangled in the forest's mane.
My wings are only a nuisance now.
Catching on branches.
And it hurts.
It hurts so much.
I don't want them anymore.
They are hurting me.

My wings are hurting me.
I cannot fly.
And just then when there was nothing left.
When I felt uselessly used.
My feet began to lift off the ground.
Light started to pour into my center.
And I saw my reflection in the forest's shadows.
I didn't have wings.
Where did they go?
All I saw was me.
And the light reflecting back at me.
I was looking for me all along.
In the things that brought me freedom.
I thought I needed wings to fly.
When all I needed was me.

The Illusion of Perfection

Life isn't always perfect.
And you don't have to be either.
You have every right to feel and think what you think.
Express it. Let it out.
Don't hold it in.
Feel the pain.
You don't have to be ashamed if your circumstance has you entangled.
Love the entanglement.
Love the crap out of it.
And watch it untangle itself.
Just because you loved it."

The Importance of Rest

When life feels light I get carried away.
When life feels heavy the last thing I want to do is try to fly and damage my wings.
So instead I rest and sit.
And listen to the thing.
And honour its weight and its load.
And love it and allow it.
To pave a new road.

Space

Everything you think is a concept pointing directly at the thing that says you're not that.

I want more freedom.
Because I'm not.
I want more clarity.
Because I'm not.
I want more love.
Because I'm not.
I want more time.
Because I'm not.
I want more connection because I'm not.

And all of these NOTS
Make KNOTS in your story.
Pinching you off from experiencing what you are.
The thing you think you are not.
The reason you chase the things to give you the feeling of

FREEDOM
CLARITY
LOVE
TIME

Loosen the KNOTS
Unthread the tension
Create space to CLOSE the gap.

And you will discover
You ARE the gap

The arrow is you pointing at you.

Amy Dawns

You are your Cupid.
You are your boomerang.

And there was never anything to close.
Only to OPEN you,
to see what you actually are.

Folding

There was never anything for you to do but unfold into love.

How does your heart feel right now?

What can you give yourself permission for now?

What can you become open to now?

What/Who can you forgive now?

What loving words can you speak to your pain now?

What do you love about yourself right now?

What is one word that you can focus on that will expand you now?

Who are you without your stories?

What does your heart need right now?

What haven't you asked for yet?

What is your true essence?

What is weighing you down that you can release now?

Amy Dawns

So What

And then my heart said, "Yes, this will expand you."
And my mind said, "But........what about all of these stories that say I can't?"
And my soul responded, "So what."

Leap

And when your heart says leap, do you leap?
Or do you walk to the edge, look down and say, "Oh Shit!"

Wanting

I want to hold back for fear of breaking.
I want to give everything for fear of taking.
I want to hide my imperfections for fear of not being loved.
I want to expose my soul for fear of feeling like I'm not good enough.
I want to leave this body for fear of being rejected.
I want to be in this body fully for fear of being disconnected.
I want to control for fear of losing myself.
I want to surrender for fear of being left on the shelf.
I want to be hurt for fear of being left behind.
I want to heal from fear of the thoughts in my mind.
I want to not say what I think for fear of hurting others.
I want to voice my insides for fear of feeling smothered.
I don't want to feel fear anymore because it feels like I haven't succeeded.
I want to love all my fears so I can feel needed.
I don't want to be needy for fear of being cast aside.
I want to be stating my needs for fear of suppressing inside.
This war is still within me. I feel unsafe knowing this.
What if it never goes away and I only experienced fleeting moments of bliss?
Can I be enough like this or will a kiss destroy me?
This is why I stay away because sometimes I don't even know what's truly me.
Today is all that matters above all.
For now I will withdraw.
Withdraw from the way I think I should look.
From all the ways I present myself like the cover of a book.
Neat and tidy beautiful pictures and fonts.
To be wanted is what I want.
The dressing up and looking pretty
is the fear of not being wanted for the plain ugly and witty.
Even my son tells me I look better with make-up on.

Soon you might be gone,
So I still use it as a mask and looking pretty becomes a heavy task.
When all I want is for someone to see my beauty beneath my skin
and let that be such a large love that my beauty rises from within.
I'm growing older and things change
One day this beauty will fade
My body a temporary vessel I get to explore life in
And for now I will mask the truth deep within with a grin.

Goddess's Garden

An awakened man would never walk into her garden and take everything he needs
for his benefit, to satisfy his greed.
Only to return and try to replant a good deed.
The awakened women wouldn't stop him, she wouldn't even heed.
Even if there was only one flower left and nothing to feed
She knows deep down beneath the soil are other seeds.
That was planted long before with the intention of becoming trees.
And amongst the forest that will grow eventually
Will be abundant without ownership of prosperity.
Take what you want; something stronger will grow.
The awakened man will always reap what he sows.

Mind Chatter

Sleepless nights
Endless dreams
Broken souls
Torn seams
Only yesterday I could see
The inner beauty
Ripped jeans
Hidden beams
Stolen light
Different teams
Fallen fool
Make believe
Monsters hide
Steal dreams
Live for love
Live for me

In Love With A Woman

I am in love with a woman.

She is kind and caring. Thoughtful and remarkably intuitive. She lives on a different level than most. She can dive deep in the waters of her emotions and meet the most exquisite nectar of her pain. She is inexhaustibly curious about all of her stories that are entangled in her perceptive below the surface. This makes her incredibly compassionate. She can be the unconditional space of love for people because she is that for herself.

I am in love with a woman.

She dances like she hasn't aged a year. Within her is a fiery majestical goddess, whose skin she wears like gold. She moves her hips as though they have told a thousand tales of what it took to become the woman she is today. Whole and complete, perfectly flawed and leaning into love the more she realizes that's all there is.

I am in love with a woman.

Scared, sometimes terrified that she will never measure up and has measured down into her insecurities just to feel a sense of safety. Still, she rises like a phoenix from the ashes each and every time stronger and more unstoppable than before. Rich in integrity, and passion spilling into every word that slips off her lips. Her words are poetry that can move into the deepest of souls. Her art can provoke those willing to wake up to their greatness. Her greatness lies within her willingness to show up unapologetically her storms and in her bounty with equilibrium.

I am in love with a woman.

Oh this ravishing lady knows her edge. She knows it so well that when she gets there, she either lays down and weeps her despair before the leap, or she rests in the overwhelming meet-cute of her internal twin flame, or she expresses herself boldly through her transparency, but she always leaps with her whole heart.

She is patient with herself. She knows she will never get it done and when she is in her finest moments of all there is, she is light on her feet. She can twirl her dress and still kick like a badass. She smiles like it's the best life she is living and laughs with her whole heart.

I am in love with a woman.

She has a heart that can extend beyond anyone's visual sight. It can reach into strangers and kiss children good night. She is the universe and the whole universe is within her soul. When you come across this amazing woman you'll know. She dreams and envisions so big that she surrenders to one by one. She gives back to others by giving them the greatest gift they could ever receive, the gift of knowing themselves deeper and truer.

She is the bridge for connection and wants everyone to know how deeply held they can feel when they begin to go within and truly listen to their own hearts and souls.

She won't stop until her very last breath, until her heart completely beats its last best chance at living fully. She won't stop raising the awareness of conscious love with everyone she meets.

Amy Dawns

The LEAP

Sometimes in the thick of the night there's this energy that keeps me awake,
Which tells me the next step to take.
And in that moment I have two choices: I can be devoted and take a bow,
Or refrain from and hold onto the fear of "how?"
When I say yes this energy moves.
It grooves,
And it dances
It's not about taking chances.
It's about taking leaps,
Into the unknown
Where all the things I don't know about me lie.
That's where life happens.
That's where I become the captain,
Of possibility.
You see,
Me is all I knew up until now.
But "I" lives in the vow,
Of my highest calling.
And you can only get there by falling,
Away from what you know.
And into what you don't.
That's where you grow
And this meditation has become an hour of poetry,
Pouring through me.
And I couldn't see,
Until I closed my eyes,
And moved into my body,
That this rhythm and these words,
Were totally and completely,
In orderly,

Precise timing.
Divinity,
Moves through me.
Becomes me.
Is me.
And I AM here,
So grateful to BE
And reality?
It can be anything you want it to be.
You'll see.
It's one of the greatest mysteries.
When you start saying yes.
To your heart that's saying,
LEAP.

Amy Dawns

The Guy That Couldn't Get the Girl

Because what he wanted to get he couldn't give himself.
So he placed her on a pedestal
And every time she fell off
He was lost without her.
Searching for her light.
Looking up where she once sat,
But not seeing her there.
He was confused and heartbroken.
He felt out of control not always being able to know exactly
where he had placed her.
His heart bleeding out for her guiding light.
Trapped in his own darkness.
So he decided to climb up to the pedestal to see what it was like.
Once he was up there he was scared, panicky even.
He thought to himself, this doesn't feel right.
I thought I would feel mighty up here, unstoppable,
like a King up here.
But instead I feel shaky, unstable and weak.
He shook so badly that he fell to the ground.
He was struck with unshakable awareness questioning, is that
how she felt up there?
He cried understanding what he had done.
He tried to contain her light by placing her always in his sight.
He turned away and as he did
There she was as bright as day.
Standing right in front of him.
What's the matter, she spoke, are you okay?
He stood staring at her glow
His awareness he could feel in his heart beginning to grow.
Yes he spoke. You're here. Not there.
She laughed, I always have been.
He stood in that spot quietly within.

As he recognized the man in the mirror with that grin.
It wasn't her that gave him life.
It was his own reflection of his light.

Amy Dawns

Take a Chance On Me

You will see
That every time you speak these words
It is a place of need.
That your inner voice is speaking quietly
Through the mouth of another
So you could hear its echo
Over and over again.
Until the suffering
Of loss and of attachment
Which you once thought was love, was in a way love, but not in
the way you think of.
It was love saying stop giving everything outside of you a chance.
And give it to the one who is always with you in the dance.
The source of what you are
The dreams, the lyrics, the visions that open your awareness.
Take a chance on YOU.

Dear Money

I feel like a failure when you're not around.
If I'm the source of where you come from then I must be lacking source.
I must be missing me?
This confuses me honestly.
Deep down I know the pain and the past longing
To understand why I still struggle.
I've been asking questions about you for years.
Sitting with you.
Shifting my awareness of you.
Showing gratitude for you.
Even spending you on things that fill my soul and expand me beyond who I was.
Paying you back.
Giving you freely.
Enjoying you.
Loving you.
And just when I feel I've shifted
I'm back here
To being broke.
And I'm thrown temptation after temptation of how I can make $600 guaranteed if I manipulate people into buying a product that I don't believe in.
And I can't bring myself to do it.
That feels worse than not having you around.
Selling my soul to a guarantee.
Yet it feels like part of my soul is so tired.
So tired of living on purpose for a purpose.
I'm not lacking passion.
I have lots of that.
I have an intention for living too.
I love my son more than words can even put down here.

I've received visions that God gave and have listened and
followed them through.
I am still doing that.
Somehow deep down I know that will sustain me more than I can
imagine right now.
I've felt true joy and bliss simply by being.
And yet there's still this cry of "Why?"
and I can feel shame with that.
Shame that I still feel the cry of WHY.
I realized the other day that Debt is the guilt of not being able to
afford something.
Getting it before being able to afford it.
Even if it was given to me by someone who could, but logically
I could not afford it at the time...There is still that subconscious
guilt inside of me.
So much awareness.
So many insights.
And yet I feel embarrassed.
That I haven't figured it out yet.
How to make enough money.
Or more than enough money.
And the thing I hear all the time is
It's our birthright to receive.
And in fact, the more we can receive the more we can actually
help people.
I've done this.
I hear the story.
Of being 43 and a single mom.
Who is brilliantly...BROKE.
"Why?" is still a cry I hear in my body.
And to be honest I part wish it wasn't there and wish it would just
fucking break through whatever the barrier is already.
I'm sitting looking at my bank account watching you leave.
Feeling in my body what it will be like to spend the last bit of you
on my rent.
And I can feel sadness that you're not here to play with me
anymore.
I feel like a child who doesn't have any friends.
I must not be fun enough.

Nobody wants to play.
Wouldn't it be fun just to play every time you were here?
Instead of being so serious about which direction you had to go.
That feels light in my body and scary.
Play money is fake.
It's not real.
Recently I would say, I am open to creative possibilities for abundance and like a magic wand something would happen that was a creative possibility for abundance.
That's not working anymore.
I'm open and ready for what's next.
And it scares the fuck out of me.
Just being honest.
I want you around.
I don't want you to be scared of me.
I want it to feel like an exhale.
Let me know when you can play.

Money Responds

It's not your fault. None of this is your fault or ever was your fault. We are so sorry you feel this way inside. It's not fair that you had to see your parents struggle so much over us. It broke you inside. It's okay to cry. It's so totally okay for you to cry all of this out right now. We totally got you. This would make any child so confused about us growing up. It's okay. It's not your fault. Let it all out. We are going to show you what's real and what's not. Take your time. There's no need to rush.

We were never here to destroy you and break your family apart. Your parents were misunderstood too. They were confused too. It's not even their fault. It's nobody's fault really. There's nowhere to point the finger and blame anyone.

This is like a big conscious bubble floating around in the universe that needs healing is all. Sounds simple enough. But it's not even your job to heal the bubble. Just be here for the little scared girl inside of you. Soothe her. Let her feel held in this space. There you go. You've totally got this. And we've totally got you. We have been supporting you more than you think and it's okay if you don't remember or can't think of that right now. It's still totally okay. You're still healing and that's totally ok. There's nothing wrong with where you are and what's happening right now. It's so perfect Amy. We are glad you took the time to write us a letter. We've been waiting for it for quite a long time. And we knew it would happen when you were ready. We support everything you do. Who you are. Who you've been. Who you are becoming. Can we show you what we actually feel about you Amy? We love you. Even when we are not around we love you. Even when you don't say thank you. Or you feel like we aren't enough we still love you. Want to know why? Because we come from the greatest highest version of you. The source of you. I know that's hard to understand. But what if you don't try. What if you feel it? We come from the source of you. I bet that feels soothing and warm in your belly doesn't it? Kinda feels like a deep connection to something you can't name or put your finger on, hey? We fill your belly in the same way. Maybe you've just never felt like this before because all you've known up until now is the little Amy who never got to cry when her parents were fighting over us. You didn't even remember that you've been holding it all inside. All of this time. That's a lot to carry around. And it's okay Amy. A lot of weight is going to go now. Weight you don't need. Fear and grief that you didn't know was there. It's all okay. We love you so very much. You're going to feel us even more now. In your belly. This deep connection to the source of you. It wasn't your fault Amy. It never was. Give yourself some time. And feel free to write to us again.

Love, Money

"No man is ever going to live up to your standards."

This post is mine based on life long experiences, searching within, sitting in my own bullshit, facing my darkness trembling like a discontented child, giving till my body felt broken and my soul shattered, a whole shit load of self awareness, consistent on-going loving myself through this whole crazy human experience and falling in love with life in layers, while simultaneously letting bricks of stories that held me in captivity be pulled out of me.

Dad, first of all, I love you more than you'll ever know and more than I've said in my 43 years.

"No man will ever live up to your standards."

Yes, my dad spoke those words to me this summer, not too long ago.
During a conversation where I was describing a little bit how I consciously show up in a relationship. And his response was, but who does that?!
And he's right you know.
Who does that?
Not very many.
A select few.
It's rare.

When he said no man will ever live up to my standards
2 things happened.
First, I felt contracted.
Small.
I could feel the little me go, "Shit, maybe I should lower my standards."

Maybe I'm not worthy of such high standards.

And the second part of me was both aware and curious of that observation.

My dad did not mean it rudely.
Not even close.
In fact, I know that it was far from it.
He wants to know I'm safe and protected.
I think all dads deep down want that in their own way.
And he knows I'm tough.
And he knows how much I've changed.
He was saying he knows I'm going to be okay with or without a partner in my life.
As a friend of mine said, dads would still walk in front of a freight train for their kids.

Here's what I know about standards for me: they are terms given to me by the UNIVERSE that support the woman I AM, the human I'm being, and what I'm becoming in a truly harmonious way.

Yes, you heard correctly.

Standards don't build walls.
In fact, they break them.
They aren't about projecting fear of the past onto the future.
They are anchored in the present moment and, yes that means they can shift, change and evolve.
They are born from love.
They know my worth and my royal heart.
They carry some non-negotiable and have plenty of space for "room to grow".
They have some hell yes's and some hell no's.
They are wild and free.
They are terms of the divine, which I received.

And personally speaking, I don't want a man to live up to my standards.
That is giving the assumption he's lower than me.

Amy Dawns

No thank you.

I would prefer him to meet my standards and love them all.
As I will meet his and love them just the same.

Love Is Still the Answer

And this whole time when I searched outside of myself for answers and healing; these things were really just messengers that I had all within me the entire time.
And that's when I decided I wanted to become the version of me that mastered the coherent energy of my heart and brain so I could continue expanding the vibration of love simply by being it. As grateful as I am that there is medicine in plants on the earth, I asked myself, what do I have to become to embody the medicine that I AM.
Love answered.
"Love is still the answer"
The love that runs through your veins is your medicine.

Power

Today I brought my legs with me.
Without a care in the world.
Leaving behind the stories of shame I once told.
They are mine and I love them
And for the first time,
I allowed them to raise me
To standards so divine.
My legs didn't define me
I set them free
I withheld from them so much love, so much that I couldn't see.
How strong they were and perfect in every way.
So I stopped all the shaming today.
Not anymore, now I hold them with love...
Above my head
And below my waist
They fit me like a glove.
These legs are mine and I brought them with me today.
This whole time they held the power of love and play.

Ambassador of Love

I sat with the world within me
I held it with love.
I listened to its blessings
From the space within and above.
It was all around me
And all inside.
It was never kept hidden
It was seeking me to abide.
With clarity it came to me
You are an Ambassador of love.
As you embody this
Your life will flourish.
It will rise above.
And you will have apprentices
That follow your steps.
Because you took the leap
Of faith into your soul.
In the core, into the depths
Where you felt the peace.
The oneness and the truth.
That this was the purpose
Of all of life's suits.
Remember, this one you once wore
You were also an apprentice before.
Stay humble; stay focused intentionally
And you will soar.
Hire these people who are seeking love
For by following your lead
They will understand they too
Are being asked to lead with love.
Remember that love is the most powerful thing.
You need not prove it is

For it is a remembering.
Do not reason with its callings
For it will reveal
All the love that is life
With its infinite power to heal.
And awaken the mighty hearts
Young and old
From the stories that speak suffering
Freedom beholds.
We will awaken.
We will rise.
We are the revelation.
We are you.
Remember what you are.
And what you came to do.
Act now with total faith, reverence and grace.
The miracle is now.
It's unfolding in every race.
The world has always been with you.
And you within it.
Share this with others who understand this.
They are the ones you are placed with
To raise the frequency of love.
You're all ambassadors
Of the universe.
With God, thereof.

Unspoken Wisdom

What you didn't know is that I am a portal to unspoken wisdom. And manipulation carries an energy that I repel. So without even knowing, I asked all of those uncomfortable questions to expose the truth. Your manipulation could never build anything sustainable, because it was based on lack. And there is nothing I lack that is pulling me towards the person I am supposed to be with.

You can't manipulate a relationship with your fears and expect it to sustain you. There was never anything sustainable except for your fears to be exposed and break apart.

Potential

Don't think for a second because I fell in love with your potential
that I didn't fall in love with you.
But I must admit,
I caught myself in a pattern
Of loving so hard that I wanted you to realize your potential.....
In order to avoid mine.

Presence

We have words written in our heart
Do you ever wonder where to start?
We have spontaneous conversations all the time
And yet I'm standing here in front of you worried that all of this
may rhyme
And, I'm wondering if I'm wasting your time.
That's fear speaking.
I wake up all of the time.
See, I said it again.
And I see myself standing on stage
Being asked to undress my soul.
To just bare it all to you
Without needing to know
What I'm going to say next.
That's courage.
And so I stand up here and with my eyes closed
I allow myself to sink into my body
To experience every cringe of discomfort and sensation.
That's presence.
And I just start speaking.
Am I enough.
How many interactions do we have?
How many conversations do we encounter in a day?
Perhaps I should have put the encounter with interactions and
the have with conversations.
It makes more sense.
Oops, stupid me.
That's judgment.

How often do we show up already judging that we aren't enough?
Like who am I to be in the spotlight and have nothing prepared.
Nothing rehearsed and yet

I apologize
That's a lie.
Because I wrote all of these words down.
When I was taken to that place.
In the stillness of my own mind
Spirit awoke me and placed me on this stage.
Speaking on the fly.
Letting whatever needed to rise
No matter what it sounded like and owning it
Or am I?
Is it even really mine?
Isn't everything that comes through us a gift of the divine?
Aren't we supposed to give that away?
Instead, I'm sure you will agree with me
We let fear have the last say.
Who am I to stay...standing up here and speak from my heart?
What if my heart doesn't actually know what to say?
What if my mind just gets in the way?
This game that we play
Inside.
We hide it well.
We keep it together by preparing
And needing to have a plan.
Or at least we think we are prepared
But we are really just scared.
While that still small voice inside of us says
I dare you
And it's daring
And for a glimpse of a moment
It makes us feel alive and free
And then instantaneously contracting us back into doubt.
And doubt demands.
STOP
Dare to be bold and big?
That's a waste of time.
Let's stay small
That might provoke something
Or worse, someone who won't understand what you're doing.
You won't know what to say next.

So why bother at all?

Fear.

Even though when I was sitting with myself these words just appeared.
And does it really matter if I stuttered and stopped?
Take a pause, take a breath
Feel the knot
In my throat
As I try to prove I'm enough
Why is having this written down proof that I'm prepared?

What if we are already prepared?
Cause I'm here. You're here.
The proof is in our presence.
You showed up!
When is that going to be enough?

I AM HERE
NOW WHAT?

Spark

My spark was so big today
My light was so bright.
Only to lighten up your darkness
You wanted to hide in plain site.

The spark you once were drawn to
Now has cast you away.
You repel the thing that made you fall in love
You will choose your way.

I will not dim my shine
Nor hide my splendour.
I will not stop my soul from rising.
Or not allow my joy to pour.

The words that seep from my lips
They are not just mine.
They come from love and truth
The very universal divine.

They are blessings of plenty
They are rich with gold.
I cannot choose who sees the brightness
From which these messages are told.

Hold nothing against the light
But fair warning when you look in.
If you're not willing
You will see your own reflection of what's hiding within.

Love Is a Focus

I once thought that love was an act of approval.
Like a hall pass that excused you from the classroom.
Like a permission slip that granted you access temporarily.

Fooled by the culture of schools and society.
I believed love was a thing you earned.

Love
It only comes with the right behaviour
The best accomplishment
The right actions
The right words
clothes.
hair.
grades.
job.
The right amount of money.
And you had better care!!!!
Cause if you don't
Love won't stay.
It will go away.

See, humans are messy.
We soak into our skin what's been laid before us.
We are marked and scarred.
We have quirks and questions.
We believe things we hear and are told without always challenging them.
We buy into the disillusion that we are not enough.
Always needing to prove our worth.
To fit in somewhere.
Sometimes anywhere.

Amy Dawns

To feel loved.

I know. I know.
When we really get honest about what we learned love is, it's disappointing.
It feels like someone cut holes in our boats and threw away the oars.
Only to find ourselves swimming in unfamiliar waters.
In the dark.
Drowning in desperation.
Drowning in hopelessness.
Drowning in broken heartedness.

But wait there's Facebook.
To give us that familiar boost.
That we aren't alone.
That we're all messed up on the ready fed, algorithm exposed cynicism of conditional love.

But I would like to challenge you.
And your perceptions.
Your beliefs.
Because we cannot escape our season that we are in.
In fact the shortcut is making ourselves even more available to it.
Not running.
Not avoiding.
Not blaming.

Pure radical acceptance.

Because here's what I've learned LOVE is.

It's a FOCUS.

We could focus on what's wrong and what's not.
Instead of what we've got.
We could focus on then instead of now.
And try to figure out somehow.
The reason for this season the world is in.

That we are in.

Or we could focus on LOVE

What I once thought love was.
Came through a filtered focus.
But here's what's cool about filters.
They alter the natural state of what you're actually looking at.
And when you become aware of this you can begin to prioritize
your focus beyond the filters.

Love is in the exposure of your filters.
Your beliefs.
Your perceptions.

Love is in the opening and the closing.
It's the blooming and the shedding.
It's also the misunderstanding and the uncertainty.
Where reason is void of this season.
And you feel lost in the dark.
Love is in the mistakes and miracles.
The setbacks and the leaps.
Love is in heartbreak and falling in love.
The marriage and the divorce.
Love is even in the worst mistake of your life and the guilt you still
carry around because you haven't let go.

Love is there.

Love is in the trauma and the truth.
Love is in every emotion and every thought.
Love is birth and death.
Resistance and Revelation.

Love is a FOCUS.

Into Me See

Ravish me with your broken pieces.
The ones left in the veils behind your smile.
Seduce me with your vulnerability.
Captivate me with your raw words that have been trapped in your veins of stories raging to surface.
Induce me with your darkness so I may transport it with my light.
Satisfy me with your fear of plunging deep down into the treading waters, containing your desires.
Hold me in your breath.
Hypnotize me with your touch, so I can feel God in every cell of my body.
Entice me as you let go, so I may find myself In the empty void of your love.
Fascinate my tongue to taste your tears that have been percolating in your lungs.

Transport me into the galaxies of wounds that make you human.
Delight me with your spark leaving burn marks on my skin, so I may embody your sacredness.
Destroy me with your authenticity, leaving me with nothing but what I truly am.
Mould me with your tenderness.
Mark me with every scar left behind, so I can come to understand the walls that were built in your heart.
Melt me with your integrity.
Reveal me to you, from your soul to your brain.

Broken Man

He has sat in my presence countless times.
Hands shaking like he has committed a crime.
Watching the boy wanting to hide.
And not be seen this way...
Weak inside.
With no words, a story that played from the energy of his body
collapsing in.
To protect and provide safety from suffering.
Feelings aren't safe.
Vulnerability is weak.
No man shall cry.
Conditioned to believe.
I've sat amongst him in this space.
I could see him wanting to hide his face.
With armour of panic and justification such.
To feel this depth of emotion was way too much.
I saw the beauty peeking through the cracks.
Where he thought he was breaking from too much slack.
He didn't want to go back.
To feeling the sensitivity his body was designed to feel.
Since he was a boy,
Deep down he knew.
And that boy was afraid he would be exposed.
As pathetic, not enough and weak he was told.
Is not how a man is supposed
to be.
Conditioned to believe.
He must always keep it together.
For the sake of feeling free.
Enslaved by society's...
Conditioning on what it means to BE A MAN.
"I Am Broken"

Words he spoke.
I sat and listened with an open heart.
I could see what was breaking,
But it wasn't him per se.
It was stories and identities starting to fall away.
I wanted to convey this,
But he wanted none.
He felt undone.
Not ready to see.
The beauty of the broken pieces that were actually setting him free.
Like a glass that had fallen and shattered on the floor.
What he once thought he was, he wasn't anymore.
He thought he was the glass holding everything within.
And once it broke he felt shattered in his own skin.
I could see the freedom in the space between the broken glass.
That was being held by some false sense of self.
The illusion that the glass was him
When he was actually the space in between the rim.
Not contained closer to experience himself more.
As true divinity, abundantly adored.
And LOVED.
He was never broken.
Only breaking away.
From the things that kept him bound, not meant to stay.
The seed that was planted long ago.
That already knew how to grow.
Into the man he was meant to become.
Everything else becoming undone.
So it is and so it shall be.
He has
Broken Free

Longing

And every time I heard our song it reminded me of what you weren't willing to become.

Amy Dawns

Sweet Surrender

There was nothing she could do anymore.
So she surrendered to the enchantment in her heart.
She lay down the whip of perfection and fell in love with her body and soul.
She looked to the moon and in it saw her reflection.
She knew that there was only this moment and this moment was alluring.

Love Never Leaves

My wish for you is when you become so entangled with the stories that your mind creates, that love calls you.
And you hear it.
Or recognize it.
May love show up in the form of a smile from a stranger.
Or a song that plays on the radio.
Or a group healing that you attend.
Or the wind that for a moment it's breeze makes you forget everything.
Or your child that laughs.
Or your dog that cuddles with you.
Or the person that holds the door open for you.
Or the setting of the sun.
Because love never leaves.
It is always there.
And just because you become entangled does not make you less deserving of love.
Love is your birthright.
You are love.
May you come to experience it over and over again in your life that one day you recognize yourself as it.

Amy Dawns

Beyond What You Know

**Out-dream yourself
Go beyond.**

Let it Go

Alignment

When she decided she was doing it for her soul the game changed.

Embodiment

She wears her body like it's the prettiest thing she's ever owned.

Amy Dawns

Dirt

She was born into dysfunction
Led by candlelight of dirt.
Each grain of soil
Every inch of Mother Earth
Molded to her body
And named it by shadows
Under-spelled by loyalty
Suffering planted in her dirt.
Disillusioned by society
Not ENOUGHNESS grows with her tall
Unworthiness becomes her
Height measures her properness small.
Dirt grows into dirty.
Dirty body parts
Dirty girl
Dirty woman
Take out the trash
Piled so high for miles you wouldn't notice that there is soil
buried.
Not enough cash
To dig her out of the dirt.
Suffocating
Choking
Trash talk that goes on inside her head
It was piled from the dysfunction she was fed.
She finds a shovel and starts to dig herself out
From the smell and the rotting of the drought.
The drowning of her fertility
And creativity at best
She started to fight for something that had been long laid to rest.
If you come across her now
You wouldn't even recognize her with your eyes

It takes a nourished soul
And an open heart not disguised.
If you see her beauty and fail to see what's behind her eyes,
And judge her dirt as insecurities
And despise
What she's done.
She will be left undone
For you to see
That what you judge is a mirror
For your own insecurities.
She is goddess
She is queen
She is woman
She is a girl
She is all that has ever been.
She is a dress that twirls.
She has taken all of the dirt that she was buried to begin with.
And created a plentiful
Bountiful estate within.
She is magical and loving
She would never point it out
That is her grace and her reverence
That she grounds in without doubt.

Amy Dawns

Whatever

Scribbles
Illegible
Caving in.
So tired
Nothing left
Questioning Everything

Brave Girl's Lullaby

May all your worries dissolve with compassion,
And your resentments be forgiven by grace.
May you sit within the vessels of your heart,
And release the need to win this race.
Be still sweet one as the nectar beckons you deep within.
And one by one breath, you will win.
The divine is all around you and is singing you to sleep.
A peaceful slumber to recharge you and take you and your everlasting companionship deep.
Let it seep into your cells, your blood, and your mind.
Let it allow you to heal and rejuvenate with kind.
It will call you by love and kindness so broad.
Here you will know that you're safe and protected from fraud.
The fraud of doubt and fear will cease to exist.
As you move into joy and happily ever after bliss.
Within your soul,
Within your heart,
Within your mind be still.
And listen ever so closely,
For the next inspired will.
You are love.
You are needed.
You are incredibly soft.
That is your gift.
This is your loft.
Curl up now and let love wrap you in its embrace.
To sleep, to sleep now.
In this heavenly space.
You will awake with young eyes and a youthful heart.
A full well of vitality to begin again, to start.
And this next cycle is calling your name.

Amy Dawns

This season.
This process will not be the same.
It is yours to receive.
Yours to allow.
Go now and be still.
This is it.
This is now.

Peace

My whole life I was searching for peace.
I disguised it with anger; that was my niche. Hidden beneath a love so blind.
Creating a war within and leaving me behind. You never know what you'll find when you look inside.
A love so kind.
How could it be you?
Until the battles have been fought and the victory won, the poppies dropped, they weighed a ton.
They turned to blood thickened quick.
And the war to your passion would stick.
TOGETHER.
Hold it together just to KEEP the peace.
So no one can see what's underneath. Come out; come out wherever you are,
Like the game of hide and seek.
Always hiding and searching for peace.
Oh there you are, within your reach.
No need to keep it together.
Just let it fall apart.
This is your moment, to begin, to start.

Amy Dawns

Heaven's Scripture

Where you see ugly, I see braille etched in scars.

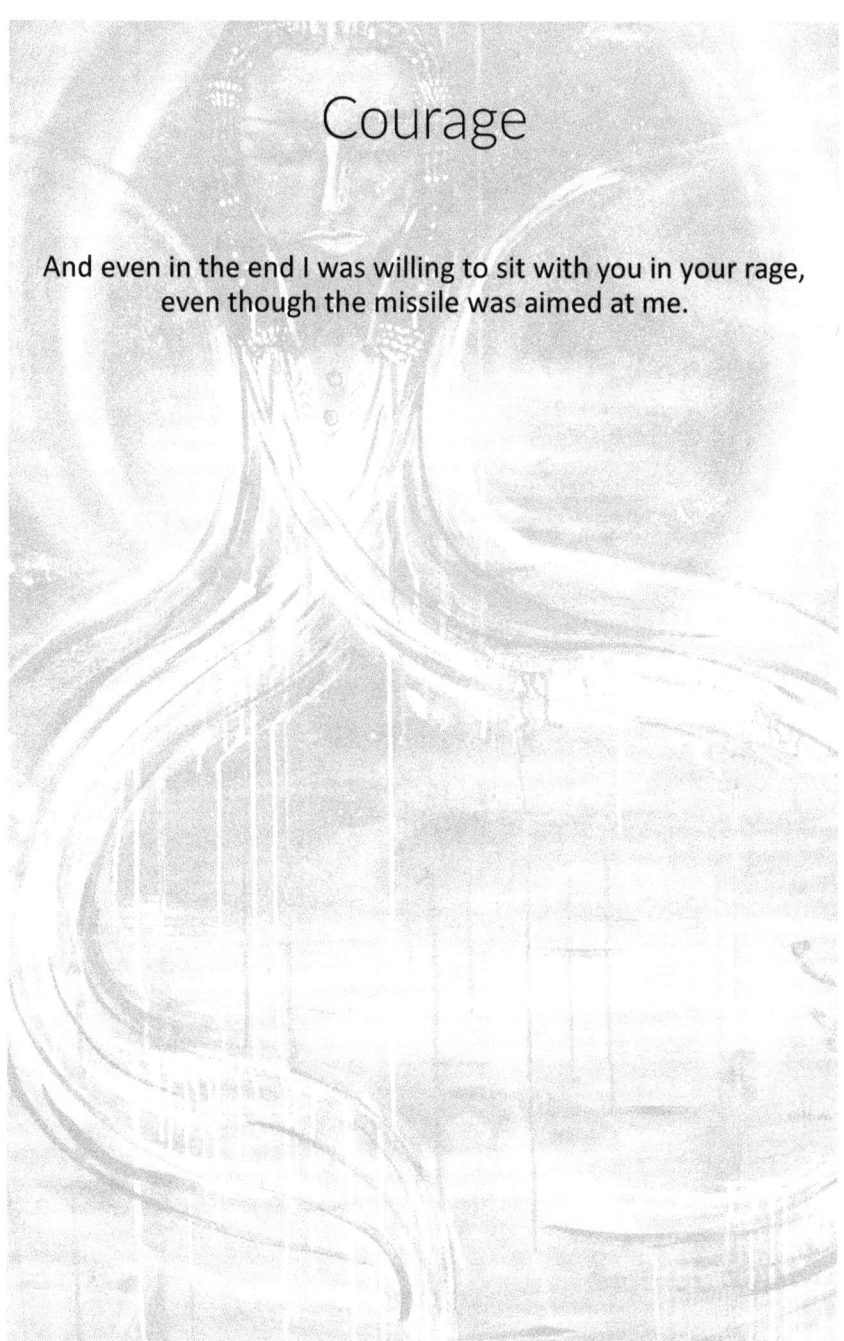

Courage

And even in the end I was willing to sit with you in your rage, even though the missile was aimed at me.

Guidance

The highest version of yourself always gives you what you need.
There is nowhere else to look but there.

Vulnerability

I showed you a piece of me before I showed it to the world.

Intuition

Intuition is like a breeze. It will go right through you. It will feel so natural you will forget that it happened.
It will feel so light you won't ever cling to it.
You don't ever have to train your intuition.
You only need to become aware of its presence and then trust it.
It will never drag you there.
It won't feel heavy.
Intuition is always free and steady.

Divine Love

Maybe once we all begin healing with love, we will softly melt this wall of illusionary entrapment between us; that we call divine masculine and feminine.
And see it for what it truly is.
We will begin to dissolve the barriers of the false sense of power and structures within ourselves, and step more and more into the truth of what we are.
The DIVINE.
There isn't a wall that separates the masculine and feminine, or male and female.
This is simply a wound that needs healing.
And the only thing that can heal it is the light and truth of love.

Coming In

When we come into the present, we begin to feel the life around us again, and we also encounter whatever we have been avoiding. We must have the courage to face whatever is present; our pain, desires, grief, loss, secret hopes, and love.
Everything that moves us most deeply.

Divine Power

I am love and light.
And my light can turn to lightning
And my love to thunder.

Deep Down

Deep Down is only intense to the one that has not gone there yet.

All she needs is love.
So she became it.

All of the images in this book are original paintings by Amy. They are viewable in full colour and available for purchase on Amy's Website: www.amydawns.com/painting-gallery

A GIFT FOR YOU

Hi.

I see you.

Thank you so much for listening to this book call you. I truly feel when things come into our lives it's because something called us to it.

As a huge thank you, I invite you to explore aspects of the greatest gift you were ever given - YOU.

As a complimentary gift to you for exploring this book, I am offering my short online course:

Awakening to the Love that Is You

It is a short read with 12 different self-love explorations you can go through at your own pace. These guides have become some of the core fundamental practices I still use to this day. They are the ones that have stuck with me the most and have been the building blocks to redeeming my worthiness, reclaiming my innocence, and restoring my sexual and sensual power (our life force energy; we aren't truly living without this).

You can receive this complimentary gift by going to this link:

www.amydawns.com/awakeningtothelovethatisyou

About the Author

Amy Dawns is an intuitive artist, healer, spiritual mentor and speaker. Amy aims to help others overcome trauma and pain. Her mission is to compel and inspire others to learn a love so deep within themselves that it liberates them from who they believe they are, while becoming aware and honouring their highest Self.

Amy lives and loves loud with courage, compassion, and a deep reverence for all of life. She radiates love as a witness to her life experiences and others. Amy serves to continuously do the inner work as she knows that is where the truest wisdom has been planted. She has learned that the "shortcut" is going within and holding space for all things to rise.

Amy has lived through traumatic experiences, sat with pain, faced it, acknowledged it, saw it and didn't run away from it. She has developed a deeply conscious, spiritual, loving relationship with her true Self and life. She continues to deepen this love and cultivate a relationship so pure and blissful within herself. Self-love has become a way of living and she is here to help others make their love loud.

Amy lives in Regina, Saskatchewan, Canada with her son and 2 dogs. She loves to paint, dance, kickbox, do yoga, and absolutely adores the vivid diversity of colour in the universe. Music moves her soul and inspires her daily to breathe life in fully.

For more information about Amy and her work:
Websites: amydawns.com or makingloveloud.com
Facebook: @amydawnsbeloved
Instagram: @amydawns1111

Have you heard of True Colours?

This moving and profound Body Painting experience offers the energy systems of the body a visual stage for expression. True Colours allows you to witness and honour your forgotten stories as they surface and become artistically realized on the naked canvas.

Deeply trapped emotions of shame, fear and guilt release you from their burden as we integrate their lessons and deliver them into Love.

True Colours sessions are photographed to capture the beauty of the stories that unfold and are revealed to you a month later to allow time for integration.

To learn more about True Colours, please visit
www.amydawns.com/true-colors

www.ingramcontent.com/pod-product-compliance
Lightning Source LLC
LaVergne TN
LVHW012109070526
838202LV00056B/5670